Lloyd Mifflin

Year-book:

Birth-days of distinguished Americans chiefly of the eighteenth century:

with quotations from the poetical writings of Lloyd Mifflin

Lloyd Mifflin

Year-book:
Birth-days of distinguished Americans chiefly of the eighteenth century: with quotations from the poetical writings of Lloyd Mifflin

ISBN/EAN: 9783337716899

Printed in Europe, USA, Canada, Australia, Japan

Cover: Foto ©ninafisch / pixelio.de

More available books at **www.hansebooks.com**

YEAR-BOOK:

BIRTH-DAYS

OF

Distinguished Americans

CHIEFLY OF THE

EIGHTEENTH CENTURY:

WITH QUOTATIONS

FROM THE POETICAL WRITINGS

OF

LLOYD MIFFLIN.

EDITED BY
E. S. B.

PHILADELPHIA:
THE LEVYTYPE COMPANY,
PUBLISHERS,

1897.

PREFACE.

In making selections from the Poems of Mr. Lloyd Mifflin, it has been thought well to confine the quotations to his *Ode on Memorial Day*, and to his *Two Hundred and Fifty Sonnets;* quoting nothing from his lyrics or minor poems.

The sentiments expressed in the quotations will be found in a number of cases to be applicable to our idea of the character over whose name they appear, but in many instances there is no connection whatever intended between the personage named and the poetical selection.

The quotation at the top of each page is intended to apply to the day of the month, and *not* to the character or event named under it. The date given is that of the birth of the character named.

In a very few instances it has been found impossible to ascertain *the day of the month* on which certain characters were born—in such cases the date has been placed arbitrarily by the compiler.

It has been the aim of the editor to include in this collection the names of many of those, who, during the Eighteenth Century, aided the cause of American Liberty and Progress.

E. S. B.

Our Heroes sleep, they rest below,
And through a thousand years,
The influence of their deeds shall go
Like perfume wafted to and fro
Around the rolling spheres.

1 . . . . ANTHONY WAYNE 1745

While still above the hill-top's wooded crest
The rosy colors linger, loath to die.

2 . . . . PHILIP FRENEAU 1752

Throned in that fine air of Tranquillity.

3 . . . . LUCRETIA MOTT . . . 1793

Gulfed in the surges of the ceaseless sea.

4 . . . . HORACE BINNEY . . . 1780

When all the pomp of fame shall fade
As fades the summer's grass.

5 . . . . STEPHEN DECATUR . . . 1779

The darling summer that we loved—in vain,
O where is she and all her gold of yore?

6 . . . . THOMAS CHITTENDEN. . . 1730

Like to the voice of the eternal sea,
Filled with a wild unfathomable moan.

7 . . . . ISRAEL PUTNAM. . . . 1718

For this is but the cradle age
That rocks the child a year;
But with the Future's tutelage
The full man shall appear.

8 . . . . NICHOLAS BIDDLE . . . 1786

Black in the zenith air,
Rose th' immeasurable mountain throne
Peak above peak of everlasting stone.

9 . . . . . LEMUEL SHAW. . . 1781

They rolled the ball of Progress up;
They took a stain from off the land;
They drank, nor passed the bitter cup;
They did the duty near at hand.

10 . . . . THOMAS MIFFLIN . . 1744

And let your heart,
Mellowed by midnight, while the back-log glows,
Touch on the themes most dear—the Muse and Art,—
Till in the east unfolds th' Aurorean rose.

11 . . . ALEXANDER HAMILTON . . 1757

They helped the Nations yet to be;
They broke a path into the skies—
For first of all man must be free
Before he can be wise!

12 . . . JOHN HANCOCK. . . . 1737

A single bell has ceased to toll afar,
And silence listens, stiller than a stone.

13 . . SAMUEL WOODWORTH. . 1785

Not so the fronts of those who live and die
Scarred with the thunder-track of Thought and torn
With eagle beaks of Art.

14 . . . JAMES GARRARD. . . . 1749

Down the dim aisles of fading memory,
Drifts the deep plaint of countless threnodies.

15 . . PHILIP LIVINGSTONE. . 1716

Some chattering snow-birds clustering on the seeds
Of winter's withered flow'rs, miscallèd weeds.

16 . . . NICHOLAS LONGWORTH. . . 1782

Through vasts unwinnowed by the wings of eld!

17 . . BENJAMIN FRANKLIN. . . 1706

Our science in his greater ken,
Shall seem a paltry toy,
As when the man looks back again
On the playthings of the boy.

18 . . . DANIEL WEBSTER. . . . 1782

Think not because upon these slopes of green
Thou hear'st no footsteps follow, that alone
I pace these vales.

19 . . . . ISAIAH THOMAS. . . . 1749

And azure seas there are, and sunset sails,
And shepherds piping on the capes of blue.

20 . . . ROBERT MORRIS, . . 1733

The snow lies white upon the frozen plain
And loudly blows the hyperborean blast;
His cohorts armed with lances of the rain
Tilt fiercely 'gainst me and go charging past.

21 .   ROBERTS VAUX.   . 1786

Elusive Spirit of the vague inane
Whose keys unlock the cavernous doors of sleep.

22 .   . WILLIAM DAVIDSON.   . . 1746

For bliss achieved is but the birth of woes,
And joy lies only in pursuit of joy.

23 .   BENJAMIN LINCOLN.   . 1733

Like young Hyperion, leaning bright
Over his cloudy chariot's side,
Let Knowledge shoot her shafts of light
Thro' crawling Error's Python hide.

24 .   . . LINDLEY MURRAY . . . 1745

And silence clings
Like some loved arm around us, long laid by.

25 . .   . EZEKIEL CHEEVER .   . 1616

A bugle's blast
Blared from the bannered turrets.

26 .   SAMUEL GEORGE MORTON.   . 1799

O'er barren hill-tops girt with windy trees
The songless thickets make their chilly moan.

27 . ROBERT YATES. . . . 1738

Sweet are the songs the soul still leaves unsung!

28 . . JAMES TALLMADGE. . . 1778

Fair faces mild with calm serenity;
The placid brows Madonna might have worn;
Clear foreheads where no cares were ever born—
These are the gauds of Youth's vacuity.

29 . . . HENRY LEE. 1756

How dear the visions which the mind's eye sees!
Sweeter the things that are not, than that are.

30 . . . JOHN HENRY HOPKINS . . 1792

I see the future temples rise
Grander than all before,
Where Man, not only free, but wise,
Shall tread this golden shore.

31 . . . GOUVERNEUR MORRIS . . 1752

The silent cypresses that fringe the hill
Bend 'neath the fury of their angry will.

1 . . . . DAVID PORTER. . . . 1780

Great ones with laurelled brows, and glorious eyes
Bright with fulfillment of their prophecies.

2 . . . . LYMAN HALL 1725

Recede, O World, and let the mysteries
Sweep in upon me of the Spirit's birth.

3 . . . . JOHN DAVENPORT. . . 1597

Dark currents whose corrosions gnaw its realm
And waste it irretrievably away.

4 . . . . JAMES G. BIRNEY. . . . 1792

Unniched among thy land's illustrious names.

5 . . . . . AARON BURR 1756

And in the sky, where all the day lies dead,
The clouded moon unsheathes her scymetar.

6   ALLIANCE WITH FRANCE . . 1778

And dream the Dawn, at last, will bring us peace.

7 . . . . . . ELI IVES 1779

Be warned! This storm is aimed at Liberty.

8 . . . . PETER FANEUIL. . . . 1700

And have you then this truth to learn,
Or do you but forget,
In times of peace
The Ballot is the soldier's bayouet?

9 . . HARRISON, 9TH PRESIDENT. . 1773

I who within the sunshine of your smile
Spread my green leaves and rapturously grew,
Rearing my towering branches to the blue
And top of heaven—which was yourself the while.

10 . . . TREATY OF PARIS. . . . 1763

But not less sweet, the winter's warm alcove,
With books and thought, and lamp-lit room, and
    scent
Of apple parings rising from the stove.

11   .   DANIEL BOONE .   . 1735

Who would not give the remnant of his days
To live one hour a thousand years from now !

12 .   . PETER COOPER .   1791

For to create is still God's prime delight.

13 .   . MATTHEW THORNTON   1714

Yes ! Safe as once were they
Feasting in Babylon when Cyrus' wiles
Drew off Euphrates, and let in his files—
His myrmidons to slaughter and dismay !

14 .   . . WILLIAM GOODELL .   1792

Serene, with dreams and fair felicities.

15 . .   ABRAHAM CLARK.   1726

Why, what forsooth, to Nature have we owed
With her sublime and callous negligence?
Nature's indifference is enough to goad
A saint to recantation.

16 . . . EDWARD SHIPPEN. . . . 1729

Without a stain upon one bar,
And in our Nation's firmament
Let Honor be the polar star!

17 . . . . JOHN PICKERING. . . 1777

Ah! but to leave,
O'er foot-worn wastes of mediocrity,
Some peak unscalable of high achieve
To daze the dim blue of Futurity!

18 . . . GEORGE PEABODY. . . 1795

The days, like some Arabian caravan,
Glide by, as still he treads beneath his trees.

19 . . . . THEODORE LYMAN . . 1792

With folded wings we paced the gorge alone,
The shining nimbus round the angel there.
Lighted my feet.

20 . . . . HUGH MERCER 1721

The sky where erst the blue
Hung her unfathomable deeps serene.

21 . Joseph Hawley. . . . 1724

When man is swept into the skies;
When systems melt away;
When time no longer onward flies;
When stars themselves are gray—
The memory of their sacrifice
Shall blossom in the skies,
And down the aisles of endless day
Go sounding on for aye!

22 . Washington. 1st President . 1732

When Day drops down the draw-bridge for the Night.

23 . . . Henry Dearborn . . . 1751

Will these fade too, and wane—
These last delusions and desired dreams?

24 . . Theophilus Parsons. . 1750

Willing, but still a martyr to my song!

25 Charles Cotesworth Pinckney, 1746

The nude white arms of the young sycamore.

26 . ROBERT FULTON. . . 1765

What is yon lower star that beauteous shines
And with soft splendor now incarnadines
Our wings?

27 . JACOB BIGELOW. . . 1787

Wings for the soul are never forged in vain,
Although the Artist and his Art be lost.

28 . MARY LYON . . . 1797

The gilded Indian of the village vane
Swirls to the east.

1 . FEDERAL GOVERNMENT EST'D.   1781

We drop on Valor's grave, a tear.

2   .   GEN. SAM. HOUSTON .   . 1793

Onward forever by thy spirit borne
Bird of the dim illimitable seas!

3 .   . THOMAS CHALKLEY . . . 1675

Ah, what a sight beneath the sky
The mountains looked on then !

4 .   . . COUNT PULASKI. . . . 1748

Safe—say ye? Listen! Hear ye not the sound
Of stealthy sappers tunnelling 'neath the walls?—
That ominous rumble heard below the ground
When muffled millions dig—no shouts—no calls,
But dark and secret workings all around.

5 . . MADISON, 4TH PRESIDENT . . 1751

Sick of the light and of the hateful sky.

6 .　　WILLIAM BRADFORD. . . 1588

Through the glooms
Loved faces throng the stairway, sweet with tears ;
And from the walls, where nothing now appears,
Each dim ancestral portrait looks and looms.

7 . . GEORGE BETHUNE ENGLISH. . 1787

The decimation of the tyrant thrones,
The fate of Empire, and the dirge of Kings!

8 .　　GEORGE CLYMER. . . . 1739

In golden summers gone and past recall
What words were whispered there of sweet and low !

9 . . . . JOHN ARMSTRONG. . . . 1795

How can the rugged Saxon which we use,
Whose roughness cleaves these lines with ragged
　　wounds,
Charm as an organ roll of Umbrian sounds
That float from Vallombrosa or Vaucluse?

10 . .　. THOMAS BUTLER. . . . 1754

Terrific roarings of Euroclydon.

11 . . . ROBERT TREAT PAINE. . . 1731

And solace with low voices not terrene.

12 . . . . BISHOP BERKELEY . . . 1684

He hopes besides—so high his wishes climb—
To leave, in the wild garden of his rhyme,
Some marvelous lily of immortal song.

13 . . . WILLIAM ALEXANDER. . . 1726

The roaring wheels of hurry on are rolled,—
This seething serpent never stops to coil.

14 . . . THOMAS HART BENTON . . 1782

Let Freedom clench her iron hand
Upon the throat of Tyranny.

15 . . JACKSON, 7TH PRESIDENT. . 1767

How beauteous with her full sails to the breeze
As slow she bends and rocks above the bay!

16   MADISON, 4TH PRESIDENT.   . 1751

Safe? ..Safe!....Why wait ye till the Castle falls!

17   WILLIAM PINKNEY 1764

, So one adown wierd pathways of the night
Hears in his sleep, by strange ethereal streams,
Music elusively beyond his reach.

18   . JOHN CALDWELL CALHOUN.   1782

At last I felt the ominous, black air, quake
With far-off beatings of their horned wings
Before they came—enormous, baleful Things.

19 .   THOMAS McKEAN. .   . 1734

I see their sabres in the air
With a sinister flash and a frantic flare,
Thirsty, and bright, and horribly bare
Fall on the foe like hail!

20 . .   COUNT D'ESTAING .   1729

Half hid in moss the first arbutus bells
Of all the year.

21 . . . CHRISTOPHER GADSDEN . . 1724

And if Man mould, he, like the potter's thumb,
Is moulded by a Force which conquereth—
That Force which swings him like a pendulum
An hour only between birth and death.

22 . . . . . JOHN HART. 1708

Where knowledge glistens like a silver star.

23 . . . . JOHN BARTRAM. . . . 1699

In everlasting anthems thunderous!

24 . . . . . JOEL BARLOW 1755

'Tis in achieving only, life is wrought.

25 . . . . WILLIAM JASPER. . . . 1750

Peal upon peal of song, that took its flight
O'er walls of sardonyx and jasper stone.

26 . . . NATHANIEL BOWDITCH. . . 1773

Beds of forget-me-nots, divinely blue,
Suddenly seen in unfrequented dells.

27 . . FRANCIS LEWIS. . . . 1713

Alone I drink this wormwood for my wine.

28 . . THEODORE FRELINGHUYSEN. . 1787

Vast shapes and vague, portentous effigies,
Stalk in the clouds and threaten,—yet men say
That we are safe.

29 . . TYLER, 10TH PRESIDENT . . 1790

O come ! ethereal unrealities,
Flood me and fill me beyond reach of dearth,
With those immortal murmurs not of earth,—
Memnonian music sweeter than the sea's !

30 . . . SIMON BRADSTREET . . . 1603

Our dead are not dead till we deem them so;
'Tis our cold hearts, alone, that let them die.

31 . . . WILLIAM BREWSTER. . . 1566

It is the Spring come back again who brings
Hope to the heart amid her daffodils.

1 . . . . BENJAMIN MOOERS . . . 1758

Make Principle instead of Craft
To rule this land of ours;
Let Politics, both North and South,
Sink their diminished powers.

2 . . JEFFERSON, 3RD PRESIDENT. . 1743

But by none else hath it been ever seen—
Only by me—and only in my dreams!

3 . . . WASHINGTON IRVING. . . 1783

One who walks close to Nature, the All-wise,
Content can live, and on her bosom, die.

4 . . . THADDEUS STEVENS . . . 1793

When in the quiet vale
About the feet. and in the far-off dale,
Close to the pool the earliest swallow flies.

5 . . . JONAS CHICKERING. . . . 1798

While gently falls again
The gracious benefaction of the rain.

6 . WASHINGTON EL'T'D 1ST PRES. . 1789

"Why pause we here?" The angel answering said,
"The journey ends. These are the Doors of Death;
Lo, now they open, inward, for the dead."
And then a Voice,—"Who next that entereth?"

7 . . WM. ELLERY CHANNING . . 1780

Making the neck of circumstance a stone
Whereon to mount, with high and haughty tread,
Up the sheer steeps to her imperial throne.

8 . . . DAVID RITTENHOUSE. . . 1732

Man is himself the great apocalypse.

9 . . . . . FISHER AMES. 1758

" Forward! no quarter!
Sabre the gunners! spike the guns!"

10 . . . . ISAAC MACKEEVER . . . 1793

At morning when the year is young and pale,
While yet the azure of the trembling skies
Is soft as is the blue within the eyes
Of some sweet child.

11 . . . . EDWARD EVERETT . . . 1794

And leave a stillness panting all around
With the remembered music of the sound.

12 . . . . . HENRY CLAY. 1777

"The road to glory is the path of duty."
A noble lesson—let us learn it of them now.

13 . . . ALEXANDER MACOMB. . . 1782

And so, for years, the conflict's rage
Reddens the white of History's page.

14 . . . . JOHN LAURENS. . . . 1753

Unload elsewhere the old-world prison vans—
Quick—to the gate!—Let the portcullis fall!
America is for Americans!

15 . . ELEAZER WHEELOCK RIPLEY . 1782

Above the rushes and dusk water-weeds
That sentinel the margin of dim meads.

16 . . CHARLES WILSON PEALE. . . 1741

Not alone
In golden voids of Heaven, but near the throne
Triumphant with flamboyant wings upright.

17 . . ARCHIBALD ALEXANDER . . 1772

The lamentation of the rose-lipped shell
On alien shores, melodiously forlorn.

18 . . . WILLIAM WILLIAMS . . . 1731

They sleep beneath the quiet skies,
In hallowed, holy beds;
The garlands of the centuries
Drop fragrance on their heads.

19 . . . BATTLE OF LEXINGTON . . 1775

Vast hollow voids, beyond the utmost reach
Of suns, their legions withering at His nod,
Died into day hearing the voice of God.

20 . . . . DAVID BRAINERD. . . . 1718

The tree tops tremble with the gentle air.

21   .   SAMUEL JOHN MILLS.   .   .   1783

As through the Void we went I heard his plumes
Strike on the darkness.

22 .   .   .   .   JAMES SULLIVAN.   .   .   .   1744

O Liberty! shed round them o'er this land
Thy beam, that they may know, and see, and hear,
The price we paid for thee was all too dear
To have thee strangled now upon this strand!

23 .   .   BUCHANAN, 15TH PRESIDENT .   1791

The Muse still sits upon her cloudy sites.

24 .   .   .   .   JOHN TRUMBULL.   .   .   .   1750

Only th' intellectual flower
That grows beyond our plucking, seems of note,
The mind imaginative will never dote
On bald lucidity.

25 .   .   .   .   .   DAVID HALE.   1791

Uprising from my feet the meadow-lark
Shook the sweet music from him to the breeze.

26 . . . . WILLIAM TATHAM . . . 1752

Young is the World, and man has just begun
To touch those havens of th' unfathomed sea
That lie enshrouded dark in mystery.

27 . . . . . S. F. B. MORSE 1791

Down—down the abysm's perpendicular,
I listened for the rock my feet had sent
Thundering, to strike some bottom.

28 . . . . THOMAS STONE 1743

And distant peoples yet to be
Shall bless them thro' futurity.

29 . . . OLIVER ELLSWORTH . . . 1745

Upon a cloud among the stars we stood,
The angel raised his hand and looked and said,
"Which world, of all yon starry myriad
Shall we make wing to?"

30 . . . . SIMEON THAYER. . . . 1737

You who were sweeter than the buds of May.

1 . . . JUNIUS BRUTUS BOOTH. . . 1796

Backward across the years now dead,
By solemn recollection led
I look o'er many a sanguine field.

2 . . . . WADE HAMPTON. . . . 1754

Land of my birth! so looking over thee
The Poet sees from his prophetic peak,
Havoc and whirlwind brewing.

3 . . . . JOSEPH HEWES 1730

Oft have I seen at eventide the thrush
Embowered in the topmost branches fair.

4 . . . JOHN JAMES AUDUBON. . . 1780

Round me at times convene
Shadows and Shades, that from their airy zone
Stand with me here upon this mountain throne.

5 . . . . JOHN LANGDON. . . . 1739

In grassy orchards blossoming all arow
Thy blooms were falling o'er the dappled wall.

6 .   . PELEG WADSWORTH . . . 1748

Anear my home in Pennsylvania lay
These Indian streams that made the summer air
Tremble with music.

7 . . . WILLIAM BAINBRIDGE. . . 1774

Let legislators, great and small,
From county-seat to capitol
Do the imperial people's will
Or at their peril fail !

8 . . . . SAMUEL ELBERT. . . . 1740

Then that dread angel near the awful throne
Leaving the seraphs ranged in flaming tiers,
Winged his dark way through those unpinioned
    spheres.

9 . . . . . JACOB BROWN 1775

Let Liberty mean Rectitude ;
Let Ignorance die alone ;
Let never more thro' brother's blood,
Red Conquest reach her throne.

10 . . . . UNION OF STATES. . . 1775

MAY

When, under the horizon far, I hear
The clarions of the dawn—how faint up-borne !

11 . . . . JOHN LOWELL, JR. . . . 1799

This Tower, by sires, for us alone was made!

12 . . . JOSEPH CILLEY 1734

Dead Tuscan by the Umbrian sea !
Thou who art dust this many a century,
What lover shall I leave to weep for me—
What wan amphora filled with woman's tears?

13 . . . ABRAHAM TEN BROECK . . 1734

Whether on the mart,
Or on the Heliconian hills apart,
Toil at thy temples builded in the sky.

14 . . . . TIMOTHY DWIGHT. . . . 1752

Waking, fails to trace or to recite
Strains he hath heard,—they lying beyond speech
In depths of incommunicable dreams.

15 . . . THOMAS PRINCE. . . . 1687

In youth how slowly passed the golden day!
As if upon the stillness of some brook
You threw a rose leaf and the rose leaf took
Its own sweet time to loiter to the bay.

16 . . . BENJAMIN CHURCH . . . 1639

England! my blood first sprang from thy dear shires—
Is it that they still beckon, or those sires
Laid 'neath thy sod before the days of Penn?

17 . . . . . JOHN PENN. 1741

Drop your garlands and your bays,
The blessings of futurity—
The benedictions of the sky,
Fall on them gently where they lie!

18 . . . . JOHN RUTLEDGE. . . . 1739

O Liberty, thou standest fair and bright,
Yet dark the threatenings round about thy head;
For there are those who hate thee—wish thee dead—
Would sink thee in the waters far from sight.

19 . . . . . JAMES REED. 1724

Kings look—and Kings despair;
Their sceptres tremble in their jewelled hands
And dark thrones totter in the baleful air!

20 . . . . . GEORGE ROSS. 1730

O happy Seed! it is not thine to die;
Thy wings bestow thine immortality,
And thou canst bridge the deep and dark profound.

21 . . . . . STEPHEN GIRARD. . . . 1750

Who nobly die, must nobly live the while.

22 . . . . ARTHUR TAPPAN. . . . 1786

Spake rashly then, but now as one who knows,—
That he who lets Love pass to clutch at Fame,
Gathers but ashes for life's sweetest rose.

23 . . . . . JOHN GIBSON. 1740

No mortal wreath, however blest,
The buried hero needs;
Immortal crowns forever rest
Above immortal deeds.

24 . . . WILLIAM DAVIDSON . . . 1746

See! From the steerage, how they scale the wall!
Awake, ye Sentries! 'Tis a Nation's call!
Shall our fair Castle sink to such base hands?

25 . . . . JOHN PATTERSON. . . . 1744

Drifting along by many a sunny nook,
Little we cared—it would ever be May!

26 . . . EDWARD LIVINGSTON . . . 1764

This is the daybreak of the Day to be!

27 . . . . NATHANIEL GREEN . . . 1742

Those splendid jewels of the soul that each
Snatches and hides forever on the beach
Of Life from Love's great tidal-wave upflung!

28 . . . . LOUIS McLANE 1786

His feet were shod with music and had wings
Like Hermes: far upon the peaks of song
His sandals sounded silverly along.

29 . . . . PATRICK HENRY. . . . 1736

Now that victory
Sits on the helmets of our enemy!

30 . . . . RICHARD SKINNER . . . 1778

And phantom squadrons hurrying to the fight!

31 . . . . . JOHN BROOKS 1752

The dells are dim with vague romance.

1 . . . . . JAMES TILTON 1745

Disdain sits on his lips; and in a frown
Scorn lives upon his forehead for a crown.

2 . . RANDOLPH OF ROANOKE . . 1773

They are the Poets—they give airy wings
To shapes marmorean.

3 . . . . THOMAS SULLY 1783

But let me live in the sweet privacy
Of my own crags and trees.

4 . . . JOHN EAGER HOWARD. . . 1752

If man is Sovereign now, who yet is weak,
What in the course of ages will he be?

5 . . . BUSHROD WASHINGTON . . 1762

One listening in the clover fields can hear
The mower whet his scythe.

6 . . . NATHAN HALE 1755

Ah, yet once more across the shadowy years
She meets me in the gloaming.   Down the lane
We hear the dropping of the pasture bars.

7 . . U. S. BANK CHARTERED. . . 1791

Then all the works of darkness being done
Through countless aeons hopelessly forlorn,
Out to the very utmost verge and bourn,
God at the last, reluctant, made the sun.

8 . . . . WILLIAM FEW 1748

Oh! like a lichen to the rock of home
Here let me cling—here sing my fleeting song!

9 . . . JOHN HOWARD PAYNE . . . 1792

Their deeds, their fame, their very scars
Shine on though they are dead,
As light that travels from the stars
After the stars are fled.

10 . . . JONATHAN TRUMBULL. . . 1710

One lies and dreams; there is no dissonance
In all the slumbering air.

11 . . . . JOSEPH WARREN. . . . 1741

The sting of this tarantula of toil.

12 . . . WILLIAM THOMSON. . . . 1727

Bend the sword and break the sabre,
Renew Thy blessed curse of toil
On this our native soil,
And give thy suffering people labor.

13 . . . WINFIELD SCOTT. . . . 1786

As the doomed Darkness backward by Him rolled
He snatched a remnant flying into light
And strewed it with the stars, and called it Night.

14 . . . . JAMES OTIS. 1702

Sceptres of youth, and manhood's diadems.

15 . . . . JOHN ELLIS WOOL . . . 1788

Enraptured by the ecstasies of song!

16 . . . . . WILLIAM JAY 1789

Therefore their names upon the shore
Of adamantine Time,
Nor waves, nor tempest's roar
Shall wash away forevermore!

17 . BATTLE OF BUNKER HILL. . 1775

Noiseless into the Nadir,—as a star
Darkened by God in anger, from afar
Drops, black, into the gulphs ignipotent.

18 . . . . JOHN WHITE 1780

Thy fate the Poet's is,—if that he soar,
He soars alone, and lonely soaring, sings.

19 . . . . LEMUEL HOPKINS. . . . 1750

Though all of Heav'n seemed turned into one lyre.

20 . . WM. RICHARDSON DAVIE . 1756

Wistâria, purpling some old whitewashed wall.

21 . . . DANIEL D. TOMPKINS. . . 1774

When from the thicket near, the quail
Pipes to his mate.

22 . . . . BENJAMIN TUPPER . . . 1738

The sun is sinking softly down the sky,
And all the air is growing hushed and still.
A tinge of rose has touched the purple hill
Where slow the silver river murmurs by.

23 . . . . CAESAR RODNEY. . . . 1730

Doth she foresee
The Seal of Doom is on her as she booms
In monstrous caverns, everlastingly?

24 . . . RICHARD RICHARDSON. . . 1704

They, from the top of their Olympian cloud,
Flung jewelled harmonies oracular,
That on the forehead of the centuries proud
Live on forever—deathless as a star!

25 . . . . ELIPHALET NOTT. . . . 1773

With slopes of bloom and beauty, and with bees
More softly murmurous than Hymettus sees
On amaranthine meads of asphodel.

26 . .   Hezekiah Maham . . . 1739

Far on the faint horizon's distant rim,
A winged spirit of the sky or sea,
How beautiful she floats, so pure and free!

27 . . . . . John Barry. . . . 1745

Dim shimmering in the heat the violet hills
Call to us vaguely from a realm of dreams.

28 . . . . James Robertson . . . 1742

Some star
Whose light a little shall prolong his day.

29 . . . . Baron de Kalb. . . . 1721

She lifts vast voices. In her awful glooms
Roar the deep thunders of eternity.

30 . . . . . James Wilkinson . . . 1757

And soft the summer wind puts by her lance.

1 . . . . . JOHN HOUSTON 1742

Lovelier to me than all Illyria's woods,
Or mythic dales Idalian, dimly blue,
With immemorial meadows sweet with dew.

2 . . . JAMES SEARLE 1730

They who create rob death of half its stings.

3 . . JOHN SINGLETON COPLEY . . 1737

Let the false statesmen have a care
How they *mis*represent
The honest men who sent them there.

4 . DECLARATION OF INDEPENDENCE . 1776

Prostrate I fell before their burning feet—
Prostrate before their flaming wing of fire.

5 . . . ROBERT TROUP 1757

The water-lilies seem to have no care
But dream on in their silence ; and the oar
Sleeps in the bateau by the sycamore.

6 . . . . JOHN PAUL JONES. . . . 1747

Those words believe not for they were not true,
That lauding other lands disparaged mine.

7 . . . ARTHUR CAMPBELL . . . 1742

Ah, not in flocks the warblers of the skies
Make the blue deeps to tremble long and loud.

8 . . . FITZGREENE HALLECK. . . 1790

Fair as in far Illyria long ago
In immemorial days divinely dim.

9 . . . . THOMAS POSEY 1750

Let me look round upon the vasts, and brood
A moment on these orbs.

10 . . GEORGE MIFFLIN DALLAS . . 1792

From upland wheat-fields, as his barns he fills,
We hear the farmer, calling to his teams.

11 . JOHN Q. ADAMS, 6TH PRES'T. . 1767

Where shall I make my grave my soul to please?
In sultry wastes where silent Arabs tread?
Upon the brow of some stark mountain's head,
Or in the lone, illimitable seas?

12 . . . . . JAMES ROSS. 1762

Out past the pickets and the tents of thought!

13 . . . GOZEN VAN SCHAICK. . . 1737

While Chaos wavered, for she felt her years
Unsceptered now in that convulsive zone.

14 . . . . GEORGE WALTON. . . . 1740

Not in these valleys where we now recline,
But far beyond the distant mountain's brow
Lies the fair land I love.

15 . . . . THOMAS SUMTER. . . . 1734

I well remember where the beech tree stood,
And how delicious was its leafy gloom
Above the cows, knee-deep in clover bloom,
With sunshine dappled as they chewed the cud.

16 . . . . GEORGE TAYLOR. . . . 1716

In amaranthine fields beyond our ken.

17 . . . . ELBRIDGE GERRY. . . . 1744

Who, with a mere incurious interest stirred,
Breaks, carelessly, some road-side rock in twain,
And startled, finds the footmarks of a bird
Imperishably printed in the stone.

18 . . . . CHARLES STEWART . . . 1778

This vapor we call Life may blind us still.

19 . . . . . JAMES MARSH 1794

Through eternity
Worlds may be born at will, but I must stay
Cold in these clouds, who beauteous was, and drew
Eös to love me every rosy morn.

20 . . . MATTHEW THORNTON . . . 1714

Across the reedy tussocks of the mere
The grazing horses send their greeting neigh.

21 . . Samuel Powell Griffitts. . 1759

It is the trysting hour, and kindly stars
Bloom in the twilight trees ..O Love! O Tears!
Oh Youth that was, that will not come again!

22 . . . . Tench Tilghman. . . . 1744

Onward he plunged, and as he came, I saw
High on his eyeless skull, a crown was wreathed;
Sceptre he held, and sword he never sheathed.

23 . . . Nathaniel Macon . . . 1757

The starry uplands of creative thought.

24 . . . . Stephen Simpson. . . . 1789

The lion people shakes its mane,
Nor will be fed with words again.

25 . . . . . Henry Knox 1750

The cattle, dreaming, stand about the bars,
Where ripe wheat yellows all the hills of June,
What time the silver sickle of the moon
Reaps down, in golden swaths, the western stars.

26 . . . . GEORGE CLINTON. . . . 1739

But War's gaunt Vultures that were lean, shall grow
Gorged in the darkness in a single night.

27 . . . . SAMUEL SMITH 1752

Recede ! recede ! all literal things that are !
Welcome the voice that is not, but that seems.

28 . . . JAMES ASHTON BAYARD . . 1767

Sole Lord of Lords and very King of Kings,
He sits within the desert, carved in stone ;
Inscrutable, colossal, and alone,
And ancienter than memory of things.

29 . . . . PETER SCHUYLER. . . . 1710

Where is the glory fled ?—where are the gleams—
The recreant Dawn's incomparable beams?

30 . . . WILLIAM LEDYARD . . . 1738

But the stone
Men heed not till it stand above his tomb—
The cold commemoration of his tears.

31 . . . . . JAMES KENT. 1763

In curtained coolness of this quiet room
With half-closed eyes I lean back in my chair,
And fanning softly, tread a land of dreams.

1 . . . Francis Scott Key . . . 1779

For he lacks wisdom, who, with mad misrule
Vexes his lake of life with Love's wild ills.

2 . . . . John Woolman. . . . 1720

And near the nibbled green
Of velvet foot-hills, watched the browsing herds.

3 . . . . Richard Caswell . . . 1729

To see thy chariot, radiant-teamed
Come up the slopes of morning from the brine!

4 . . Jedediah Huntington . . 1743

What hopes! what fears! what rapturous sufferings!
What burning words of love will there be said!
What sobs—what tears! what passionate whisperings!
Under thy boughs, when I, alas! am dead.

5 . . . Thomas Lynch, Jr. . . 1749

Warbling her love-lay in the golden air,
As on her beating breast the sunset flush
Lay like a glory.

6 GULIAN CROMMELIN VERPLANCK, 1786

Words of great Poets, pure as peaks of snow,
Should stand up through the ages.

7 . . JOSEPH RODMAN DRAKE . . 1795

Passionate cravings for some moorland fen ;
For furze, and rowen, and a heathery glen.

8 . . . . . JAMES BOWDOIN, . . . 1727

It was the sweetness of thy lips beguiled
Life of its pang and made the darkness bright.

9 . . . JAMES CLINTON. . . . 1736

A tree will prove a blessing all life long.

10 . . . EDMUND RANDOLPH . . . 1753

So silent is the air, so hushed, so mute,
That e'en the sentinel heron does not hear,
But stands erect, nor drops his lifted foot.

11 . . Theodric Romeyn Beck . . 1791

I see the cannon mow them down
Like mowers mowing hay.

12 . . . Francis Marion. . . . 1732

And calmly hears
Love's surges beat against Life's lessening shore
As on a land that he shall touch no more.

13 . . . . Francis Barber. . . . 1751

And holds the blue of heaven calm and still.

14 . . . Peter Buel Porter. . . 1773

Hearing a voice that calls me o'er the hills,
Rise and walk onward, with no fear of ills.

15 . . . Benjamin Hawkins . . . 1754

While, 'mid the silences throughout the day,
The locust's sharp staccato stabs the ear.

16 . . . EDWARD G. MALBONE. . . 1777

Come up into the mountains, and be free !

17 . . . . DAVID CROCKETT. . . . 1786

And in mute marble see the immortals bloom
Down the long aisles of gilded galleries.

18 . . . WILLIAM MACPHERSON . . 1756

And 'tween two worlds, 'tis thou that canst let fall
The cloudy drawbridge of Daedalian dreams.

19 . . . MICHAEL RUDOLPH . . . 1754

Within the Muse's realm a denizen
He walks at times with wingèd feet elate.

20 . . . . CHARLES FRASER. . . . 1782

I hear the ecstatic song the wild bird flings,
In future summers, from thy leafy head!

21   .   ASHER BROWN DURAND. . . 1796

The satyr pricked his goat-ears, wonderingly,
And dropped, atween his hoofs, his pipe of oat.

22 . . JAMES KIRKE PAULDING . . 1779

Comes she from silken Fez or dusk Cathay,
With scents of sandal-wood that round her play
In all her sails?

23 . . OLIVER HAZARD PERRY. . . 1785

Why should I like the restless, ever roam
And clip the world from shining shore to shore?

24 . . . JOHN MORIN SCOTT. . . . 1730

Thou sweet inexorable Poesy.

25 . . . . . JOHN NEAL. 1793

While in a dusty glory all the cows
Come winding, slowly, up the golden lane.

26 . . . THOMAS PYM COPE. . . . 1768

To thee much have I owed
Sweet Idleness! whose wings are always furled.

27 . . . . . JOSEPH REED. 1741

And roam these hills, far inland from the sea !
For after health, what better hath this life
Than Rest, and Thought, and sage Tranquillity.

28 . . . . NICHOLAS FISH . . . 1758

Thy tortures have I borne,
Thy vultures, thunders, lightnings, and commands,
Yet thee I still defy—defy and scorn !

29 . . . . RICHARD RUSH 1780

Still does Apollo down the scarlet ways
Of sunset glory charioteer his team.

30 . . . . . JOSEPH DENNIE 1768

Watching through green trees
Some host of far-off clouds, that slowly soar!

31 . . . . DAVID HOSACK . . . 1769

Who marks the glint of wings in woodland ways—
The gold of flickers, and the blue of jays?

1 . . . . CHESTER HARDING . . . 1792

May move as peaceful as a folded sail.

2 . . GILBERT STUART NEWTON. . 1795

And many a caravan
Halting at wells twixt Cairo and Kairwan,
Hearing the birds, believed in Psapho's line.

3 . . . . JOHN SCUDDER 1793

Beyond *that* future still I look,
And with the Seer's eyes
I read, as in an open book,
The final prophesies.

4 . . . WILLIAM THOMPSON . . . 1781

Then War shall doff his plumes of red,
And Conflict's flag be furled ;
And universal Peace shall spread
Her white wings o'er the world.

5 . . . . FIRST CONGRESS. . . . 1774

The pendent garlands of the garden hops
Sway with the breeze ; and the blown peach tree
    drops
Her globes of crimson in the grassy lane.

6 . . . . . LAFAYETTE. . 1757

And on the void's black beetling edge, alone
Stood with raised wings, and listened for the tone
Of God's command to reach his eager ears.

7 . . . . THOMAS HARTLEY . . . 1748

Across the years the phantom waves of green
Boom at its base above the petrel's screams.

8 . . . . EDWARD TYNG. . . . 1755

I stand against the gods for man alone.

9 . . . . ELEAZAR LORD. . . . 1788

Lift me above; and thou once more be mine
Far in the bosom of thy clouds of gold !

10 . . JOHN JORDON CRITTENDEN. . 1786

Beloved dales, and crags that touch the sky,
The tendrils of my heart for years have grown
Around you all—ye cannot be o'erthrown,—
Ye hold my heart, and shall until I die!

11 . . . . FELIX GRUNDY 1777

We rest supine; we listen to the roar,
And bear the slow abrasion of the tides.

12 . . . WILLIAM VAUGHAN . . . 1703

But I will make my soul a pool, and seek
The sheltering hollows of the hills afar.

13 . . . . CASPAR WISTAR. . . . 1761

Torch-bearer to illimitable glooms
And cavernous hollows of impending years!

14 . . . . JOHN HARVARD. . . . 1608

The novelist's cockle-burr of dubious seeds.

15 . . JAMES FENNIMORE COOPER. . 1789

And faint is heard and low
The pipe of some brown Faun beneath the pine.

16 . . . . WILLIAM GORDON. . . . 1730

Still soaring heavenward with unwinnowing wings
Lose thy dark self in realms of dazzling light.

17 . . . . SAMUEL HOPKINS. . . . 1721

They pass the sea and all its snowy foam,
Its vast and restless rolling and its roar;
Mountains and vales, dread deserts they explore,
And glorious cities dim with many a dome.

18 . . . . DANIEL DENISON. . . . 1613

High on the mountain, brother to the cloud,
I stand upon this elemental stone
As free as kings upon their native throne.

19 . . . . WILLIAM GASTON. . . . 1778

He of the thyrsus and the vine,
Comes with his leopards and his skins of wine.

20 . . . . CHARLES CARROLL . . . 1737

Yet in the heart the fragrance of the rose—
The summer's rose—lingers with eloquence.

21 . . . . SAMUEL HAMMOND . . . 1757

O Sorrow, Mother of melodious Woe!

22 . MARSHALL PINCKNEY WILDER . 1796

Enough for me the brook's
Sweet counsel, and the torrent's roar.

23 .   . . ISAAC REED. 1778

Beyond the narrow verge of space and time.

24   . TAYLOR, 12TH PRESIDENT. . 1784

Place me on high above the Cataract's shore
Amid the mists, the sunshine, and the gloom;
Still hearing, in that immemorial roar,
The thunder of God's presence round my tomb!

25 . . . . JAMES MUGFORD. . . . 1725

Then from the turrets on the ramparts lost
The Twilight cohorts flaunt their flag of gray.

26 . . . ABRAHAM WHIPPLE . . . 1733

They cannot die.
Indelible and permanent
Their deeds are written on the firmament—
Be ye content!

27 . . . . SAMUEL ADAMS. . . . 1722

Their sob dies with them, like an untolled bell.

28 . . . . JAMES WARREN. . . . 1726

In upper rooms
I hear faint foot-falls, silent for long years;
Lost lips bend down anear me.

29 . . . ZABDIEL BOYLSTON. . . . 1680

I feel the zephyr's breath that here and there
Bends the poised arrow-heads, and interlocks
Gently, their barbs.

30 . . . WILLIAM SHORT. . . . 1759

.

Who's this a-coming through the mellow haze
Nude as young Bacchus, russet-skinned, embrowned;
His brow with clustered grapes and grape leaves
    bound,
And trailing vines of scarlet all ablaze?

    1 . . . . Rufus Choate 1799

     And still with its irrevocable strides,
     Tramples the sea upon us evermore.

    2 . . . . . Junius Smith 1780

     Then drifted down the gateways of the sun
     With fading pennon and with gonfalon,
     And cast her anchors in the pools of gold.

    3 . . . . John Rodgers . . . 1771

     Hands laid in ours; dear faces once caressed
     And left forever.

    4 . . . . Thomas Lloyd. . . . 1649

     A splendor merged into the infinite;
     A glory now forever passed away.

    5 . . . Jonathan Edwards . . . 1703

And hear from hill-tops dim the baying hound.

6 . . JOSHUA REED GIDDINGS . . 1795

And seas new made, immense and furious, each
Plunged and rolled forward feeling for a beach.

7 . . . TIMOTHY MATLACK 1730

I knew her by immortal murmurings:
'Twas Psyche, white-limbed, glowing like a star!

8 . . . . . JOHN CLARKE 1609

A million years are as a day
In Thy omnipotence!

9 . . . . . LEWIS CASS 1782

The sculptor, unillustrious and alone,
Pent in the still reclusion of his room,
Carves, through the vexed vicissitude of years
Some marvel in Carrara.

10 . . . . BENJAMIN WEST 1738

The light is going; but low overhead
Poises the glory of the evening star.

11 . . . . Philip Turner. . . . 1740

Kingdoms in ashes, past them all she flows,
And dust of monarchs and swart queens she dooms
To lie along her sands.

12 . . . Bartholomew Green. . . 1666

How could the spirit dare to set in speech
The poignant love that lies beyond the reach
And utmost eloquence of human tongue
Upon the shores of Silence.

13 . . James Mitchell Varnum. . 1749

Look down with patience on the lesser men
That thou hast left behind thee, and their ways.

14 . . . . . William Penn 1644

To Vallombrosian valleys let them go;
To steep Sorrento, or where ilex trees
Cast their gray shadows o'er Sicilian seas.

15 . . . Thomas Hutchins . . . 1730

He dozes near the cider-press for days,
Sipping the oozéd juice of pomace lees;
And leaning on the cope of orchard walls,
Watches the golden apple till it falls.

16 . . . . NOAH WEBSTER . . . 1758

Beloved Poesy! to thee I cry . . . . .
Wrap thy dear arms around me—hold me strong!
Oh! wake me with thy kisses when I die!

17 . . CHARLES ROBERT LESLIE . . 1794

O had I but thy wings when storms arise,
Grey spirit of the sea and of the shore!

18 . . . TAPPING REEVE 1744

The thunderous breakers capped with agony.

19 . JOHN ADAMS, 2ND PRESIDENT . 1735

He loved His darkness still, for it was old:
He grieved to see His eldest child take flight.

20 . . . . . JAMES LOGAN 1674

Now, like a red leaf on the autumnal stream,
That cannot steer nor stop—that cannot sink—
Swiftly I drift.

21 . . WILLIAM HENRY ALLEN . . 1784

'Tis nature's error when two lovers die.

22 . . DAVID BRADIE MITCHELL . 1766

Slave on 'neath Life's insufferable load.

23 . . . . THOMAS PINCKNEY . . . 1750

Comfort, O Hope, the while we draw this breath;
Be near, and lead us with exultant wings;
Aid now,—we shall not need thee after death!

24 . . EDMUND QUINCY 1681

Ah! there is but one—
Autumn, that drowsy Faun, who slowly steals
Down through the woods away—and all is dun!

25 . JOHN PENDLETON KENNEDY . 1795

Delay awhile, delay O sinking light!
A little longer linger in the sky.

26 . . . . . AMOS STODDARD. . . . 1762

The dim aureola of the western glow
Lingers above the river hill-top's rim,
And the sweet huntress, now a virgin slim,
Draws, in immortal fields, that silver bow.

27 . . . . STEPHEN OLNEY. . . . 1755

The fields are pages, and their leaves, divine.

28 . . . ALEXANDER MURRAY. . . 1755

Delude me into dreams that have no end
Until I feel—it is not Death, but Sleep.

29 . . ROBERT GOODLOE HARPER. . 1765

In that unfooted dim dominion
Beyond aurorean reaches of the sun.

30 . . . . ZADOCK PRATT 1790

The beggared monarchs of a realm of tears!

31 . . . . JAMES LOVELL 1737

NOVEMBER

A stately figure walking through the wood ;
Her features faded ; in her eye a tear.

1 .   STEPHEN VAN RENSSELAER. . 1764

Bird of the wave! my soul, as thine, is crossed
By the same spirit of undying quest—
Far on the shoreless ocean of unrest
Driven forever, and forever tossed !

2 . . . POLK, 11TH PRESIDENT. . . 1795

Apollo still is cruel as the sea.

3 . . WILLIAM CULLEN BRYANT. . 1794

Their deeds, their fame, their very scars
Shine on though they are dead,
As light that travels from the stars
After the stars are fled.

4 . . DECLARATION OF RIGHTS . . 1774

Dreams are in sooth, the only verity.

5 . . . WASHINGTON ALLSTON. . . 1779

How still the groves ! And has some silver flute
Ceased suddenly ?

6 . . . . John Barnard . . . 1681

And o'er her vast and ever-shifting floor
Thou, on thy grey wing roaming, still dost soar,
Forever drawn to where the distance lies.

7 . . Silas Horton Stringham. . 1798

The aching nation holds her breath,
And Silence stands and listens, still as Death.

8 . . . . . William Wirt 1772

Across the distant times unborn
That sleep in gloom enfurled,
The mystic veil aside is torn—
I see the ending world !

9 . . . . William Linn 1752

The stars, that up the gentle evening's slope
Through amaranthine meads of heliotrope,
Tread on imperial, haughty and supreme,
Shod with those sandals of eternal beam.

10 . . . . James Wilson 1742

What did it matter all the mud and slush?
What did it matter should love bring us pain ?
Your voice was like the gurgle of a thrush—
Your voice that I shall never hear again !

11 . . Peyton Randolph . . . 1723

In late November when no skies are clear,
When the great splendor fades from all the vines,
And no last leaf the wood incarnadines.

12 . . . William Maxwell . . . 1798

From o'er th' empurpled gravel of the bar,
Faint to us comes the lonely bittern's scream ;
While on the darkening mirror of the stream
Falls the effulgence of the evening star.

13 . . . . John Dickinson. : . 1732

Some sleep below, but memories oft they bring
Sweet as remembered odors of the hay.

14 . . Noble Wimberly Jones . . 1724

That purple pomp Egyptian, long gone by.

15 . . . . Baron Steuben. . . . 1730

There is a beauty gone from out the day;
There is a planet fallen from the night.

16 . . . . FREDERICK MAY. . . . 1773

And sipping, softly, hear the hiss and foam
Of beaded bubbles bursting round the brim.

17 . . . . DAVID KINNISON. . . . 1736

And in life's turbid wave, forevermore,
Drops the crown jewel of his Melody,
As one who from some cliff upon the shore
Lets fall, unseen, a ruby to the sea.

18 . JONATHAN MITCHELL SEWALL . 1745

Her crimson robes that long the winds withstood,
Now trailing torn and dark throughout the year.

19 . . GEORGE ROGERS CLARKE . . 1752

A phantom ship across the sunset strand
Rose out of dreams and clave the purple seas.

20 . . . PEREGRINE WHITE. . . . 1620

The low sad wail
Of scentless winds that scour the bitter vale
And find no fragrance now from all the meads.

21 . . . . JOSIAH BARTLETT. . . . 1729

Then Darkness trembled and began to quake
Big with the birth of stars, and when He spake
A million worlds leapt into radiant light!

22 . . . . PHILIP SCHUYLER. . . . 1733

Her face the grave of beauty, sad, severe;
A queen dethroned and in her solitude.

23 . . . EDWARD RUTLEDGE . . . 1749

Enough! and let our poor words cease.
Our strongest praise in feeble breath
Made superfluous by Death.

24 . . . . DANIEL MORGAN. . . . 1736

The pensive Muse,
Secluded from the world, by willowy banks,
From immemorial times has loved to stray
Along the murmuring margin of fair streams,

25 . . . . HENRY SARGENT. . . . 1770

NOVEMBER

And now portentous phantoms fill the sky.

26 . . . . . John Sevier. . 1745

It was the sweetest silence ever fell
Upon the ear of earth.

27 . . Artemas Ward . 1727

The still solitude
Became a harp whereon his voice and mood
Made spheral music round his haloed head.
I spake—for then I had not long been dead.

28 . . Stephen Higginson . . 1743

There is each day a melancholy tone
Tolled from the cloudy towers of sunset red.

29 Benjamin Chew. 1722

From the dim sea's unknowable extreme.

30 Lawrence Kearney . 1789

66

Far—far the naiad of the brook has flown,
Her reeds are tuneless on the icy shore;
Gleams from the wood, white as Carrara's stone,
The Dorian column of the sycamore.

1   WILLIAM SHEPARD.   . 1787

Ah! no assaulting bands—
No hounds of Care swarm at the gate and bark.

2   . RICHARD MONTGOMERY .   1736

The music of the saw-mill when it sings.

3   AARON OGDEN. .   . 1756

There was a time when o'er my gentle books
Upon the vellumed treasures and their lore,
From morn to trancéd midnight would I pore.

4   WILLIAM NORTH   . 1754

A voice which came from regions high, far hence,
Making rosy all the sky
With its beneficence.

5   VAN BUREN, 8TH PRESIDENT   1782

What memories tender of the long ago
Moan through the lyre of these limbs and fall
Soft on the heart and with their sighs enthrall
The lonely soul until the tears o'erflow !

6 . . . . Eleazer Oswald. . . . 1755

The blind Bard's book was open in my hand,
There where the Cyclops makes the Odyssey's
Calm pages tremble as Odysseus flees.

7 . . . . . John Morton 1724

So as man's night comes on, fain would he weave
His name around some deathless star, or die
To give it to a flower.

8 . . . . . Eli Whitney 1765

Far through ethereal fields, and zenith seas,
High, with strong wing-beats and with eagle ease.

9 . . Arthur Middleton . . . 1743

Idealize To-day, then carve your Dream,
Your ear held closer to Life's red heart-beat !

10 . . . Matthias W. Baldwin . . 1795

Then leave that buzzing hive, the city mart;
Come, while my gnarl'd oaks hold their wealth
    of snows,
Come to a country hearth.

11 . .   Hiram Paulding. . . . 1797

I see the prairies blossom wide
With million happy homes;
And where the buffalo herds abide,
Uprise the gilded domes.

12 . . . . John Jay.   . 1745

O Time! despoiler of the dreams of youth;
Iconoclast! with the cold heart of Cain,
Killing our pleasures for us—all! in sooth—
Even the pleasures of remembered pain!

13 . . . . . Ambrose Spencer . . . 1765

Leaving the rude Cathedral of my Song
Unfinished still—devoid of spire or dome.

14   . Return Jonathan Meigs.   1740

This being made, He yearned for worlds to make
From other chaos out beyond our night.

15 . . . . John Haviland. . . . 1792

Gray tangles of long grasses, sere and pale;
The flowerless stalks of most pathetic weeds.

16   GEORGE WHITEFIELD. . . 1714

Take all that is, but leave me all my dreams,
That solace like the presence of a star.

17   DEBORAH SAMPSON . .   1760

Their rancor is not cured, but only cowed.

18 .   HUGH MERCER   . . . 1721

Whoso shall lay his hand upon the lyre
For twice a hundred times, as I have done,
Needs must reverberate some earlier tone,
And often strike, alas, the selfsame wire.

19 .   BENJAMIN TRUMBULL.   1735

No long-drawn caravan across the sand,
With camels carrying silks of Samarkand ;
No dancing girls with anklets tinkling clear,
Nor troop, nor scymetar, nor pluméd spear.

20   THOMAS WILLING . . . 1741

T' endure that Fate we cannot comprehend,
And like the Year, submit, and learn to die.

21 . JAMES EDWARD OGLETHORPE . 1698

The idle—worthless—pauper—renegade,
Swarm on the moat. Shall Europe—Python foe—
Slough her skin here? Arise! and tell hèr, No!

22 . WILLIAM ELLERY. . . . 1727

Tier upon tier of seraphim, bedight
With most excessive glory.

23 . THOMAS MACDONOUGH. 1783

Trudge round life's circles still, with willing feet;
And from the sheaves of trial and of pain,
By patience strong, and by endurance meet,
Tramp out, ere evening comes, the golden grain!

24 DR. BENJAMIN RUSH. 1745

And He was agéd ere the thought of morn
Shook the sheer steeps of black Oblivion.

25 JOSEPH PALMER 1788

71

And on the high crags where the wan snows freeze,
The gaunt gray Winter mounts his stormy throne.

26 . . . . THOMAS NELSON. . . . 1738

O Thou, who art the God of Peace,
No less than God of War,
When shall the Nations' carnage cease,
When shall arise Thy star?

27 . . . . NATHAN DANE 1752

Why do we sing? Alas! because we must.

28 . CATHARINE MARIA SEDGWICK . 1789

Bring Thou all war unto a close ;
Let Peace resume her right ;
The battle field shall bear the rose,
And Wisdom spread her light.

29 . . . . JAMES NICHOLSON. . . . 1737

But if the dark days ever come
When holy duty calls,
When man must leave his quiet home
To storm a foeman's walls,
Be sure, O War! that thou shalt find,
Though scattered far and wide,
Ten thousand hearts they left behind,
As brave as those that died.

30 . . JOHN EDWARDS HOLBROOK. . 1794

Hush! for the Day is kneeling down in prayer.

31 . . . . EDWARD HAND 1744